Pledging

For

Success

To my fav Cuzn Chris
You helped inspire this book
& for that I say thank you!!!
Now Dream Bigger!!!
5'4"11"

Eric Lee Usher

Editing/Typesetting: Carla M. Dean, U Can Mark My Word

First Edition

ISBN: 978-0-578-08465-7

Printed in the United States of America

Acknowledgements

I am truly blessed to have had so many powerful individuals assist me in this process. Thank you.

Introduction

Success is your desired outcome that will provide you joy, fulfillment, and prosperity. Your vision of success is unique to you and your life experiences. Imagine a future of peace, happiness, and success designed just for you, and how that life would feel. Consider your most important goals that you wish to conquer. Now, take a moment to close your eyes and picture yourself in that moment—that moment of bliss. The moment when you can say you have all you have ever wanted in the palm of your hands. Now, ask yourself how you are going to get to this ultimate point in your life.

I will guide you through a step-by-step process on the journey to success. You will be given key life skills that will enable you to prosper in all of your endeavors. Please do not let the word success intimidate you, because it is a personal definition that each person has to define. Being successful is accomplishing that one thing that will make you feel complete, alive, and free. It will provide you happiness and peace. Let go of the concept that success only applies to becoming a billionaire. *Pledging for Success* is about what your dreams are and how you can succeed at grasping them. In this book, we are going to focus on the general meaning of success. No matter how big or small the goal is, the importance is measured by you.

This pledge process can apply to the farmer whose main goal is to grow a field of crops, the student who wants to earn their degree, the mother that strives to be an ideal parent, and yes, those who want to become singers, dancers, actors, CEO's, etcetera. You name it. Success is anyone's goal. Anyone's desire that is self-fulfilling holds positive energy and will reap positive results.

Pledging for Success will be your ultimate guide through your pledge process. Each chapter focuses on a different unique element necessary to cross over into success. I will guide you through your research, your personal reflections, your blessings, and even your setbacks. Affirmations follow each chapter along with several motivational stories throughout the book to keep you empowered. Think of these pages as your map that will lead you through your journey to success. At any point you hit a stumbling block or need an extra push, here you will have the necessary steps in your hands to continue to thrive.

Once you have completed your pledge, you will have the inspiration to continue on your journey. You will find newly discovered confidence within yourself and be able to accomplish anything in life. Those of you who complete this pledge process successfully will have a sense of empowerment knowing there is a step-by-step process to anything you want to accomplish. Goals will no longer be intimidating to tackle because you now have the tools and the knowledge base.

Everything great in life has to be accomplished through a

process, one that each step is approached meticulously and with passion. In order to take these steps, you have to make a dedication to your dream and make an oath to yourself to accomplish it. Make a pledge to you and your goal—a solemn promise until the end. Together, let's make a *Pledge to Success.*

Chapter 1
The Pre-Pledge

A successful individual is defined as one who has the attainment of wealth, position, honor, or the like. The journey to success is a very personal experience and can only be truly defined by the person embarking on the journey. Once the commitment to succeed has been made, the most important thing to keep in mind is that your experiences along the way are unique to you and your goals. The experiences on your journey will lead you to be a better person and provide you with the strength and wisdom to achieve your endeavors on your way toward success. Personally, I have experienced many things and learned a lot from my journey toward success that has lead me to be the man that I am today.

While still in college, I had a window of opportunity to become successful as an insurance broker at a young age. Little did I know the experiences I gained as an insurance broker would prove to be one of the biggest lessons I would learn towards becoming successful.

When I was just in my early twenties, my business partner and I were contracted to sell life and health insurance products across one of the largest cities in America. The company proposing to partner with us had the best quality insurance products available for health and life insurance policies. During our final meeting with the partnering company, we were informed of the huge market for these products in Houston, Texas, and urged to open an office there. My business partner and I were so ecstatic about this opportunity that we decided to take a leap of faith and left Atlanta.

After the meeting, the move to Houston took place less than a week later. We evaluated the profit of the move and the success the business would provide us. Then we put our faith in everything, deciding to risk it all! We were so sure in our goals that we arrived in Houston without neither a place to stay or an office. Driving extensively around the city, we searched for places that were fully furnished and available to move into quickly, but we had no luck. At this point, we were slightly frustrated but still stayed positive, keeping our ultimate goal in mind.

When it was time to extend our rental car lease, we noticed a building across the street with a sign reading *Space Available*. We walked in only to find out there was a beautiful, fully furnished highrise overlooking the city, and it was available that day. We felt so blessed to have found such perfect housing in such a short period of time. Once the paperwork was processed, we were completely moved in within just three days. Our minds were put at ease knowing we had secured a place to stay. Although, oddly enough, our luck had not ended yet. Just down the street, we found a perfect office for our new business that was within walking distance from the condo. All of this was like a breath of fresh air for us; we were elated with the blessings we received. Things seemed as if they were happening for us out of nowhere.

Next, we began hiring and training individuals, and started to duplicate the system we had in Atlanta into our new office. This initial process took a few weeks, but it was necessary in order to give the business the strong foundation it needed to succeed.

We were on a weekly payment schedule and expecting a deposit from the insurance company for our first commission check of ten thousand dollars. One day, while on the bus on my way to New York for a training seminar, I called my bank to see if any deposits had been made. The bank confirmed that, as expected, the first check had been deposited. My heart felt as though it had dropped into my stomach when I heard my account balance for that one week's payment. That feeling was one of the best moments in my life that I will never forget. It brought so much joy to me that it's almost indescribable. There I was, only twenty-two years old, with a house in Atlanta, a highrise condo that overlooked downtown Houston, and a profitable insurance business that my partner and I ran out of our own office. I felt as if I was on top of the world. I was living the good life.

Then another unexpected event took place. We moved from Houston because our partnering company in Atlanta informed us that we may be contracted to do some major insurance deals in Louisiana. The project would have netted us hundreds of thousands to millions of dollars. I was thrilled; I couldn't believe the blessings that were pouring in. Being excited, we made the transition to Louisiana in a matter of weeks.

However, first, we had to pass the test to attain our Property and Casualty insurance license, which would allow us to sell homeowners, auto, liability, and commercial insurance products. Once obtained, I would be a property and casualty insurance agent and be able to sell products that protect both individuals and large businesses from financial losses. This license would extend my business capabilities greatly and bring in many more contracts.

The license was the only requirement left to obtain in order to provide these policies and secure the contracts we wanted. We were certain things were going to continue falling into place for us. We were *so* certain that we began shopping for cars, penthouses, and new suits. The life I once felt was out of reach was now mine. I felt like a new man all over again.

We studied day in and day out for a month to pass our licensing exam. All my focus was on passing that test, and when I did, I felt as if my whole life had changed. I felt that I had reached the pivotal point in my life where I could provide for my mother as I have always wanted to and give freely to my family and friends. Little did I know, there was a different plan for me.

Once I passed the test, I expected to receive and sign new contracts immediately. I also expected this to be the easiest part of the transition. Unfortunately, we waited months for contracts to come our way. We became worried, but were slightly relieved every time we heard business was coming soon. We eventually exhausted all of our funds with the hope of receiving these contracts. However, they never came. Just like that, all of our hopes and dreams were shattered. We spent our money based on a dream that hadn't quite become our reality.

Our partnership eventually became bitter, and we ended the business. I moved back to my home in Atlanta and was at the lowest point in my life. I stayed at home all day doing absolutely nothing. My phone got cut off, and I felt like I had no contact with the outside world. I felt absolutely miserable. My mortgage payments were months behind. My mother began to nag me, trying to convince me that I needed to do something with myself besides sitting around, but I was so down that all I could focus on was my hopes and dreams which had been shattered and snatched right out of my hands.

I went to a crossing for my fraternal organization where the guys became members of my chapter. I noticed the difference in emotion from the moment they crossed (meaning the journey had ended) to the moment they were still enduring the process. It hit me then that if I went through this process with my organization, there was nothing I shouldn't be able to do. I had to swallow my pride, put aside my ego, and get a job— something I, the insurance broker, thought I would never have to do.

In this book, I will lead you through your own journey to success by sharing the experiences I learned when I hit rock bottom—having absolutely nothing to my name except debt— to where I am today. During that most important time, I learned you must have a process and a desire to push forward. Donald Trump said it best in his book *Why We Want You to be Rich.* "A goal without a process is just a dream." Sadly, many people do not have a process.

I created this book because I noticed a similarity between a fraternal pledging process and the process most take on their journey to success. This chapter explains the pre-pledging process. The pre-pledge is where it all begins. It's the beginning of the thought. The pre-pledge allows you to ensure that the pledge you plan on making is what you truly want. Websters defines a pledge as "an oath, solemn promise, or agreement to do or refrain from doing something. To make a pledge is to promise solemnly or formally or give as a guarantee."

The pre-pledge tests whether or not the process you are about to embark upon is the one for you. In many cases, you cannot make a pledge without first knowing what you are committing to. In the pre-pledging phase of your journey, you are most naive. You are unaware of what to expect. You may be forced to make some changes that you normally wouldn't want to do, but in order to even begin a journey, you want to make sure you've packed your bags with everything you need. Here are five essentials that need to be in your bag:

1. **Have an open heart and mind.** Be willing to accept what comes. Without an open mind, your judgment may be cloudy. It's always best to start new things with a clear heart. Your conscience should be your guide. Follow the exercise at the end of this chapter.

2. **Drop your ego.** Learn to put it aside. Our ego can stop us from doing the things we need to do. You have to master your ego or you won't be able to master yourself. This will be further explained in later chapers.

3. **Be willing to take risks.** No reward is gained without risk. How can we learn without first trying something ourselves? You can have calculated risk, but it's still a risk nonetheless. Don't be afraid to conquer your fears. By doing so, you're forced to grow.

4. **Learn to cooperate.** Nothing can be done alone. Have you heard the saying "teamwork makes the dream work"? This is true when involving anything. You will need someone's help, so learn to be cooperative. I'm not saying you have to like

everyone, but learn to work with the people you may not like.

5. **Decide to have fun.** I would hope we all know how to do this. During this process, having fun is usually the last thing on your mind, but you must try to see the beauty in chaos. In doing so, you are bettering your life and health. The joy that laugher brings can be one of the best vitamins for your body. When you're happy and having fun, you tend to feel better about your situation.

Consider this part the first step. The fact that you were willing to start speaks volumes, now you have to prepare yourself for the pledge you are about to embark upon.

Exercise: Learn to Meditate. Meditation is one of the best ways to clear your mind and allow answers to flow in. A great way to meditate is to block out about fifteen minutes from your day and find a nice, quiet place where you feel comfortable. Make sure to have on comfortable clothing and close your eyes. Focus on your breathing. Take deep breaths in and then slowly breathe out. Only focus on your breathing. At first, you may not receive any answers, but in time, you will notice a difference. Just do it with the intention to feel good, to have a moment out of your day when you can relax. As you do this on a daily basis, you will notice the change and clarity you will feel in your life.

Affirmation: *I am a powerful person able to do powerful things.*

Chapter 2
The Research

Now that you have decided you want to make a pledge and are serious about enhancing where you are, how do you decide which organization or field you want to pursue? For the lucky few, their goal is given to them in the form of dreams, inklings, or talents that let them know the path they should take. For others, it is taught by experience or a sudden awareness that takes place in that person's life. In many cases, you have those who are surrounded by mediocrity and have not been exposed to something greater than their environment. For them, the goal is realized the moment they decide they want something different than where they are.

This chapter will explain the importance of research and give some key pointers that will get you started. No matter what prompts or drives you in the direction of success, please know that in every endeavor or new adventure, you must do your research. Research is extremely vital because it provides an in-depth understanding of the topic or field of interest. For example, a businessman is required to fly to Asia to sign a new client. He believes he does his research and studies Korean dialogue and customs. Upon meeting, the client greets him, but the businessman learns that the client is Japanese. It is one thing to go off what you *think* you know, and it's another thing to completely understand it.

When you're really passionate about something, you become curious. You want to know more, and that wanting to know more gives you the motivation to do the research. Doing research is actually the fun part of the process because you get to learn more about whatever you're trying to achieve. You become increasingly more knowledgeable. Before you take a trip anywhere, you must know where you are going.

First of all, let's get rid of the notion that research means going to a library for hours and pouring over encyclopedias. For example, let's say you want to be a lawyer. Not only will you study hard, but you will also place yourself in a lawyer's environment. Research is questioning, learning, and being around the people who are in that field. If you have chosen the right area for you, you will willingly want to know everything about your passion. You will find yourself being drawn to the area of your passion. You will be highly surprised by what you will find once you decide to get to know everything about your dreams.

Another example from my personal experience is that for years, I wanted to be an image consultant. I felt it would develop into a passion of mine and that I would succeed in this industry. My form of research was the internet, of course, and talking to people in the field. Upon speaking with my cousin Chris, he advised me that professional image consulting is a lot more than what it appears to be. He advised me if I didn't have a sincere passion for fashion and clothes, I should reevaluate my pursuit. He explained that piecing together someone else's image is a lot more difficult than it seems because, in addition to understanding the client's wants and needs, you have to know their type of environment, what's important in that environment, what's considered to be offensive, what the norm is, and so on. Basically, after doing some simple research, I realized that image consulting was more in-depth than I had assumed and that it was not truly the path I wanted to go down.

Research gives you a more realistic perspective from what you may have already been told or what you currently believe. It provides truth about an area. Would you want to launch into the area of your dreams with myths and misconceptions, or would you rather go into that area knowing the truth so you can be fully prepared for your journey?

Research can have different components. In order to find an answer, you must first have a question. However, the key is to start asking the right questions. If you are ever lost about what to ask, always start with who, what, when, where, why and how? We all have heard these, but the most important question to ask is WHY? It's the single most important question that will lead you to your how. **If you don't know *why* you're doing something, then the *how* will always seem impossible.**

There's an exercise I was taught while going through the millionaire mind intensive training created by T. Harv Ecker. We wrote a big WHY on a sheet of paper, then wrote a question at the bottom, and depending on the topic, we had to ask ourselves WHY over and over until the WHY was so emotional that it nearly brought most to tears. My question was why did I want to be an actor. After asking myself why over twenty times, I came to a conclusion that allowed me to see clearly how it was going to take place. The point of this exercise was to express the fact that when we have such a deep connection to something and we are clear about what it is, our HOW is not far from logic.

There are other ways to research, as well. You can utilize the internet; there are many sites that cater directly to your needs. Another great tool is to befriend a person who is knowledgeable about your interests and concerns. Go to a bookstore and look up books that are in your point of interests. The primary key to doing research is you have to want to learn more about that given topic. You have to become a reporter and dig deep to find what you're looking for. In many cases, you will be pleased about your findings, but you may even discover that it may not be for you. **Nonetheless, you will never know until you find out.**

On your journey to success, it is very important before moving forward that you know exactly which direction you're going. I can't stress this point enough.

Exercise: Do the research. For the next one or two weeks, allocate one hour a day and strictly focus on the topic, field, or position that you want to pledge in. Create a Word document that will allow you to copy and paste as much information as you want. Then organize this into subtopics. That way, you will have all you need in front of you. I promise that as long as you do the research, you will uncover the answers needed to guide you on your pledge to success.

Affirmation: *I am not afraid to ask the questions I want to know the answers to.*

Chapter 3
The Interview

Now that you have done the research, it's time to make your decision known to the universe. In any field or line of work, once someone decides they want to pursue a goal, they must go through an interview process. By choosing an arena and pursuing that goal, you are jumping into the circumstance that you want to be a part of. **Reveal yourself to the world that you want to operate in.**

This chapter has a two-part meaning to the word Interview. Yes, I'm referring to a physical interview, such as for a job, an audition, or anything that stands between you and your pledge. Also, the primary meaning I want to focus on is the *Inner View*, looking from within. This is when we take a personal assessment of our current situation. It's been said by many gurus that "YOUR INNER WORLD EFFECTS YOUR OUTER WORLD." What you constantly think about over and over again will eventually appear in your life. Because of this, always be aware of the thoughts you allow in your head.

When going to an interview, the main objective is to be

selected. Once interviewed, two things can happen; either you get accepted or you get denied. If the circumstance accepts you, you're on your way. If not, do you consider it a failure? Do you move on to something else? Or do you remember your pre-pledge and why you made it, and then continue your journey?

The interview process, not in the literal sense in life, is one of the most important aspects of the journey to success. This is true because oftentimes life does give us a "no". Just as an initiate for a fraternity or sorority can be told no, we can be told no in many aspects of our life, and quite often as well. It's similar to when a business owner gets denied a loan request or an actor doesn't get the part he or she auditioned for. Sometimes when you reveal your intentions to a circumstance after the interview, you can get rejected. It's a part of the journey. If we were easily accepted by everything we went after, we wouldn't strive for anything, thus having no purpose.

However, this is a defining moment. Either you can give up or you can look into yourself and find something to learn from that experience. Perhaps you were not fully prepared for the opportunity. Zig Ziglar states, "It has been said that success happens when preparation meets opportunity."

BEWARE OF THE EGO! The human ego is the enemy to the *inner view* process. Oftentimes when we get rejected, we have a tendency to blame the situation, our family, our boss, and so on. The ego will tell you, "Don't worry about it. If they can't see what an awesome guy/gal you are, it's their loss." And it is so tempting to listen to the ego, nurse our little wound, and give up on our dreams.

If you are making a sincere pledge to success and believe that what you are seeking is your purpose, do not take a rejection as a setback. Take it as an awareness that says you may not be ready yet and you need more preparation. If a person has a true pledge for success, they will put their ego aside, try to learn from the experience, and see how they can better prepare themselves to move forward. **Beware of the Ego, the human ego.**

The INTERVIEW is an opportunity for an individual to get an INNER VIEW of themselves. You get a VIEW WITHIN the situation, but most of all, you get an INNER VIEW of yourself.

My freshman year in college, I auditioned for a lead role in *Oedipus*. I was quite confident that I would get the part and was sure of my talent. I felt as if I would be the ideal Oedipus; there was no way possible I wouldn't get the lead role. The reality is I didn't get the part. I got a supporting role, and this left me quite disappointed and confused. It was at that moment that my ego stepped up and offered me tons of reasons why I didn't get the part, none of which had any reflection on me as a person. All the blame was on someone else. However, it was at that moment I decided to look past my ego and get an INNER VIEW of myself. I learned a lot. I found areas where I could improve and worked hard to do so. A year later, I got the lead role in *Hamlet*. Having done the lead role in *Hamlet*, I can honestly say that back when I thought I was prepared for *Oedipus*, I really wasn't. I couldn't have handled a lead role in a play, but had I allowed my ego to take over, I would never have taken an INNER VIEW of myself and learned what areas I needed work so I could be properly prepared. This was my INNER VIEW in my journey to success. What is yours?

Exercise: Get a blank sheet of paper and put yourself in a situation where you are at YOUR interview stage in life. Write yourself a note that you will not let your ego get in the way. On the left side of the page, write down ways in the past how your ego has stopped you. On the right side of the paper, write how you could have performed an INNER VIEW OF YOURSELF and learned from the situation. Think of at least one thing in your life that your ego got in the way, and you looked within to overcome it. A good example is when a good friend of mine was fired from his job and everything in him wanted to blame the company. After he did a personal assessment, he discovered what he had to change within himself to sustain the next job.

So, now you have gone through the interview process in your journey to success. Some of you may have to go through this process more than once, but if you go through it correctly and continue to remember and honor your initial pledge, you will eventually get to what you are seeking and hear a YES! When that opportunity or situation tells you YES, it's a time to celebrate because you have begun the journey to your success. You are taking the next step in meeting your pledge for success. Once this happens, it's like all this time you have been forming the snowball of your dreams, and you have now pushed that snowball down the mountain to start collecting. Experience knowledge as it moves in the direction of your dreams.

At this time, you will find you begin to change as you move toward your dreams because it becomes real to you. Your thoughts and habits change because you are now in the race. The snowball is rolling now; the process has really begun.

Affirmation: *I will not stand in my own way. I will learn to control my emotions and rise above my ego.*

Chapter 4
The Pledge

What is a pledge? By definition, a pledge is an oath, solemn promise, or agreement to do or refrain from doing something. To make a promise solemnly or formally or give as a guarantee.

Since we were children, we have been taught to take pride in pledging our allegiance to the flag, or an organization, or a religion. But what about making a pledge to self? If you could make a pledge to yourself, what would it be? It is important to take time and ask yourself what you want. Oftentimes, we focus on what's best for the next person, but the most important person is you.

I remember the first time I flew in a plane. I asked my mentor why is it that prior to takeoff they state to put on your mask first before helping anyone else. He replied, "If you're stuck in your seat and I pass out trying to help you first, what good am I?" A lot of us live our lives not understanding this simple concept. Making a pledge to self is the best thing you can do for YOU. How significant would this pledge be in your life? Would it be just words from your mouth, or would it have a deeper meaning and conviction that will continually anchor and inspire you on your journey to success?

One of my great friends, Vincent, had many passions while going to school. One of his main goals was to join a fraternity. Due to uncontrolled circumstances, he was unable to complete his goal at the time, but the pledge was already made in his mind. There was no turning back for him. Years passed and he still showed support to the organization with hopes of one day becoming a member. It wasn't until he decided to go back to school after starting a family that he had another opportunity. Vince just so happened to attend a school that didn't have a chapter. (Each school is categorized by chapters to distinguish the many different groups.) He was able to become a part of history by chartering a chapter at the school and being a founder at that chapter. Not only did he become a member, but he will forever be a legacy of his organization, being the oldest member to have chartered an undergraduate chapter. Vincent had a personal connection to his pledge. He was emotionally vested, so nothing could tell him it wasn't going to happen.

This is a slightly dramatic example, but the point I'm making is you must have an emotional connection to the pledge you are making. If you do not have an emotional investment in your goal, then your chances of success are narrowed. Emotional attachments to our passions inspire success, because true happiness is found through our emotions. As proof of the importance, consider the fact that all of our best memories can be recalled through emotions.

Throughout this chapter, I will ask a series of questions that I want you to reflect on. It has been taught that questions hook the mind. So, pay attention to the first thought that comes to mind when reading these questions. What do you think you bring? Why do we fail? Why do some people succeed in accomplishing their dreams while others do not? Are any of us better than the next? Do those who succeed deserve to be successful more than others? The key to any form of success comes from within the individual striving to reach their goals. These questions are important because in many cases I have heard others compare themselves to one another. You have to start taking accountability for your actions.

The truth of the matter is that you can be the best or the worst thing that has ever happened to your hopes and dreams. The deciding factor is the commitment to your well-being. At first glance, you might say, "Of course, I'm committed to myself!" But, let's look deeper into the nature of a true commitment.

Place your hand over your heart and say, "I pledge allegiance to me, to do whatever it takes to be the best me I can be." Feels good, right? However, what does it really mean to pledge? What does it mean to pledge for oneself? What does it mean ultimately to pledge for success?

A pledge is the strongest commitment one can make to self. So, let me ask you again. Are you truly committed to yourself? Are you willing to make a real, convicting pledge to your success and allow that pledge to anchor and encourage you through life? If so, then you are already on the way to becoming the success you have dreamed.

What drives you to pledge? Is it because you feel this is what you were meant to do? Perhaps it's because of your desire to succeed, accomplish your dream, or fulfill your passions. What is your dream? What is your passion, and where did it come from? Do you believe that the area of your chosen field/endeavor is what you are supposed to be doing to have a successful life?

I believe God has assigned his dream to the dreamer, meaning that the desires and passions you possess were instilled in you from the beginning. Whether a factory worker or a CEO, if it's your dream, it's your dream for a reason and just as important to the design of your life. Everyone has their personal pledge in life, and you decide whether to take that journey forward or leave the pledge as a mystery. Either way, you will always think about it. It is a part of your DNA. An unmade pledge for success will always somehow be in the back of your mind as a missed opportunity. It is very important that you strive not to have opportunities, but strive to have experiences.

Making Your Pledge Real

Anyone can say that they are committed to success, but to actually take your dream and commitments out of your head and put it on paper, it makes all the difference in the world.

Pledging for success is much like casting a spell. Just like the spellcaster will come up with what he or she wants to happen, you as an individual must come up with what desires and dreams you would like to see play out. A spell doesn't become powerful until it is written down, and it doesn't become true until someone verbalizes and acts out the steps listed in the spell.

Now, let's come back to the real world. When you write down your pledge, you make your dreams real. You make it tangible. You take something from inside your head and place it on an outside object so it can be clearly seen. By writing down your goals and your commitment to those goals, they are released into the atmosphere and can be made known to the universe.

A personal pledge without a deep, emotional, or meaningful conviction is no pledge at all. That being said, no matter what area of expertise, a deep commitment to your goal is required for you to succeed. A pledge is what drives you to continue your task and not give up until it is completed.

A pledge is less about *what* or the *how*, and more about the *why*. Why are you starting a new business? Is it because someone else told you it was a good idea? Or because when you lay your head on your pillow at night, you can't stop thinking about creating something that is not only an extension of you, but can provide for you, as well? Do you want to be an actor to be famous? Or do you act because of the joy it brings you every time you step on stage?

Making a pledge for success is about taking your *why* and letting it inspire you in such a way that you find yourself making a real commitment to do whatever it takes to reach your goal. You have done the research and moved beyond the Interview. It's now time for you to make your Pledge. Take time with this process, this can be considered your personal mission statement. Make sure to attach emotions that you can always draw up. This will be your reference when you lose sight.

Exercise: I encourage you to take time and create your pledge for success. Use the space on the next page. Recite it, hide it in your heart, and make it meaningful for you.

Affirmation: *I am my greatest investment. I truly commit to myself and my well-being. I pledge allegiance to my success.*

My Pledge

On this day, my pledge for success is:

_____

_____

_____

_____

_____

_____

_____
Your Name

_____
Witness's Name

_____
Date

Congratulations! You're on your way.

Chapter 5
Predetermination

So you have launched out into the area of your dreams. You are excited. Things are happening. You are learning more about yourself. You can see your dreams on the horizon. You're going to change the world, right? Exciting, huh?

Now, let's be real. If you are at this stage in your journey to success, you have probably encountered some setbacks that you did not anticipate while you were celebrating being accepted after the interview process. For example, you might be working long hours, not seeing the sales you expected, or getting some negative feedback from friends and family members. Whatever the case, LIFE happens, and you realize that the process of reaching your dreams can leave you burnt out, tired, disappointed, and unsure.

PLEASE READ THIS SLOWLY. Regardless of your pledge, you WILL encounter setbacks on your journey. Be prepared. It WILL happen. Things get hard; life starts to weigh on you. It is a part of the process. In this chapter, we will explain why and show you how to elevate your mind and overcome your obstacles.

Just as in a fraternity or sorority, the pledging individuals eventually reach a point where they must go through a serious process to "cross". (Crossing is when you've accomplished your goal. You have received what you were seeking crossing over.) It is during this process that the pledging individual begins to question their motives. Did they choose the right organization? Who told them this was a good idea in the first place? Is this really what they want to do? Is it too late to turn around? What will people think of them if they give up?

This point is crucial in anyone's journey to success. When you step out into your dreams and get your butt kicked by circumstances of low sales, low energy, marital problems, financial issues, late mortgages, etc, you have a serious decision to make. At this point, you have established your dream, made a pledge to reach your goal, done your research, decided to announce your intentions to the universe, and then taken the big leap into your desired field. Now you are in it. Now you are a business owner, an actor, a realtor, etc. The rubber has hit the road, and you start to hit struggles you did not anticipate.

Again, I say *there will be moments when you feel like giving up*. This is the time to remember your pledge and why it was made. Realistically, once things go wrong, some people say, "You know what? It's not supposed to be like this. I must have made the wrong decision," or "I can't take this. This isn't what I signed up for. I'm pulling the plug."

In the pursuit of success, people do give up. They get tired/worn out and quit. That's just life.

For those of you who know that this is your purpose and are still facing adversity, this is the time to stay focused. You must know that the point of your success is already predetermined.

Now, let's go back to the pledging process. When a person passes the interview stage and actually starts the process needed to move forward, the fraternity or sorority knows from the moment an initiate begins the process exactly when they will finish. In a sense, their moment of success is already predetermined. However, the initiate has no clue when their test will end. All they know is that they are on a journey and hope to eventually crossover.

The organization, knowing exactly when an initiate will cross, then puts the individual through a number of tests and trials to provide an opportunity for personal growth and appreciation of the organization. This process tests the individual's will and reveals their true motives.

The same applies to your situation. When you launch into an area, you must fully believe that you will be a success. You must believe that God timed the evolutionary process of your success. The only thing between your start and finish is *time*. Within that time, many things take place that leads you to your pledge. Remember, the snowball is rolling. In any journey, time serves as a buffer to give us the necessary experiences we will need to maintain and increase our success once we attain it. The success has already been predetermined, but it is up to the individual to go through the process to reach their goal.

This is important. If you do not believe your success is predetermined, you should stop pursuing your goal right now. It's the belief that we will succeed that keeps us pushing forward. The dictionary defines predetermination as something that is determined in advance. As explained in this book, I want you to walk away with the belief that your success is predetermined. It is in belief that we put our trust in the outcome. Why else would you start a business, establish a nonprofit, or write a book if you didn't truly believe you would eventually reap the benefits of your labor?

For those of you who say if success is already predetermined, what about the people who fail and never reach their goal, success can be measured in many different ways. The beauty of predetermined success is that we base our beliefs on what we want to achieve, which gives us the willpower to keep going. The reaching of a goal is a choice. Point blank. We may not know the plan that is in place, but we can choose to believe the outcome will be rewarding. It is in believing that we live.

I remember my first corporate job after I left the insurance industry at the Autotrader.com headquarters. The transition was hard for me. I was forced to ride public transportation to get to work every day, and then I bribed people with food for a ride home from the train station. I was a part-time employee, so I didn't make enough to purchase a car. Months later, I was promoted to full-time employee because of my sales.

As a part-time employee, I didn't have to be at work until six, so my daily routine was finding someone to bribe with food or gas to take me to the train station. However, now as a full-time employee, I had to be there every day at 8:00 a.m. I remember telling my boss that I didn't have a car but had been looking—the irony working at Auto Trader. My manager reminded me that when I started full time, I would need to get to work on time or else the position would be given to someone else.

With only two weeks before my full-time position started, I went to a "buy here, pay here" car lot. They had a car that I'd had my eye on for some time. Since I now had a full-time income, I would easily be approved. I was told by the salesman that with a thousand-dollar deposit, the car could be mine. The following week, I got paid and returned with a thousand dollars to attain the car. However, when the salesman sat me down, he stated the loan office needed an additional five hundred dollars in order for me to drive the car off the lot that day. When you're on a fixed budget, that's a lot of money to give. I was forced to come back the second week. I had no choice. It was either get the car or lose my promotion.

I came back to the dealer with $1,500 ready to get my car. My salesman wasn't there, but the manager told me that he had left a note stating I needed $1,700. I was done! My goal of getting a car was over! I stormed out of there mad as ever.

My friend Irvin, who was with me, tried to calm me down. I got over it quickly, though. I just let go and figured maybe it wasn't meant to be. We went back to his apartment where his roommate was playing videos games. We started laughing and joking about the whole situation, when his roommate remembered that his professor was selling a car. We met with him the next day, and he sold me a 2004 PT Cruiser limited edition with 43,000 miles and in good condition for one thousand dollars. I was able to drive to work that next day.

My goal was to get that car from the lot, which would have resulted in me having to make car payments every month for the next three years. The vision God had was for me to get a car that I could afford and that fit my current lifestyle. We may have a specific goal in mind, but the ultimate goal will be predetermined by God.

God grants each of us the freedom to pursue our respective goals; He determines our point of success and allows us to run the race any way we please. It is up to us to decide whether we will get tired and quit or finish.

The same is true for Kelvin Davis, the oldest professional

rookie in the world. As a teenager growing up in Evergreen, Alabama, Kelvin set his sights on becoming a professional basketball player. Before finishing high school, he was granted a full scholarship to Alabama State University. His talent and drive to play pro-basketball fueled him to break school records and lead his team to multiple championships. All signs pointed to the pros.

However, at the height of Kelvin's basketball career, his life took an unexpected turn. He accepted God's call on his life and became a minister, placing his basketball career on hold. Though Kelvin became a pastor, father, and husband, he never fully gave up on his hope of one day being a professional basketball player. He is quoted as saying, "When something is in you, it's just in you. No amount of time can ever make it go away. It's like you can't rest until it's done."

Twenty years after leaving the sport he so loved, Kelvin Davis decided he was going to accomplish his dream. At age forty-seven, he announced to his family and friends that he was going to play pro-basketball. To his surprise, his family was overly supportive; however, those outside his family questioned his sanity and assumed he was experiencing a midlife crisis. Unfazed, Kelvin continued to pursue his dream, committing himself to rigorous workout routines that often pushed his limits and challenged his commitment. The story of Kelvin's journey began to spread, and the media latched on to him, following him to practices and interviewing those close to him.

In August 2007, Kelvin Davis showed up at the ABA tryouts for the Atlanta Vision, the oldest man ever to set foot on the court for a tryout. With his unbelievable ability to outleap, outreach, and outscore his drastically younger counterparts, Kelvin made world history when he was asked to become a member of the Atlanta Vision, making him the oldest rookie in the world. His success in this area created a whirlwind of interest in the professional basketball world. Donning the name given to him by his younger teammates, Old School Davis made his mark in history and finally reached his dream. When countless reporters asked him what made him think at the age of forty-eight that he could accomplish such a feat, he responded, "My faith in God. If He says it's gonna happen, it's gonna happen. Doesn't matter if it takes five years or fifty years. It's going to come to pass."

I like this story because it shows that circumstances of life will cause goals to change and situations to be altered. It also shows that committing to something you want may lead you to a happy, even though not original, ending. Also, this is a renewed goal, because he lived his life and achieved goals before altering his dream about basketball and finally being able to achieve professional status. The pledge we make is based on where we are now in our life, and as we persist, the pledge will have additions to it. However, the ultimate goal is to have a pledge to believe in.

Exercise: Let's have fun with this exercise. Go back to the days as a child when you had a big imagination. Now, wherever you are, focus on something that is in your grasp, right in front of you. Look at that object. Once you have the object stamped in your mind, I want you to close your eyes. I want you to create a destination where you can go or where you can touch something that is available at that moment. I want you to visualize yourself making a move to touch this object that you know is there. I want you to see yourself touching that object in your mind and really feel complete that you were able to touch it. Visualize that. Now, I want you to actually go touch the object at your physical reach. The important thing is to follow exactly how you visualized it in your mind. This example may seem simple and elementary, but once you understand the process you just created, you will be amazed. This is how you act on a daily basis. A successful journey has already happened. You just have to go through the physical motions of it.

What is the difference between you visualizing and touching the object and when you actually touched it? Write it down. Your answer will reveal how you think about goals.

The interpretation is this: If you say the difference is you actually grabbed it, that means you're the type of person who says, "I'll believe it when I see it." Yet, in the journey to success, it's actually just the opposite. When you start to believe it, that's when you will see it.

If you say there is no difference, then you've got it. You can evoke emotion just by thought. Just like with nightmares, you can feel every emotion while you're asleep as if it was actually happening. Nothing is different besides our perception. Use this exercise as a mechanism to help you concentrate on thinking and visualizing you meeting your goals.

Affirmation: *I am where I am, and it is okay.*

Chapter 6
Unexpected Support

So now that the snowball is growing, you are in your area of expertise. You have faced some challenges and you've decided to push forward. This is about the time wonderful things will begin to happen. Support comes from unexpected sources. Have you ever had something happen that seemed completely coincidental, but worked in your favor? That's similar to what we are discussing here.

In this chapter, I will discuss why not to confuse what seems to be a well overdue outcome with the final goal. In other words, don't confuse the light at the end of the tunnel as being out of the tunnel already. Support can mean any form of help or contribution; here, it is used as a sense of accomplishment. Don't get me wrong. It is a great feeling when you receive support, but it's not over yet.

In many cases, when support comes from unexpected sources, you can begin feeling like you have succeeded. This is when it can feel like success has happened and that you have finally reached your goal. During the time when other people begin to acknowledge and support your dream, you begin to feel that finally after all the small setbacks, there is finally a light at the end of the tunnel. You start to feel like success is right around the corner. It is similar to when a recording artist gets signed to a label. While the artist may feel like they have finally made it, the truth is that the journey is just beginning. Don't let this fact discourage you; this step is required for true success to take place. Let me stress that unexpected support is only intended as a tool to keep you going. Its primary purpose is to show us that we are on the right path. Still, you have to persevere throughout your journey.

My younger sister, Ameena, had a passion to work in the film industry, so she decided she wanted to take a leap of faith and move to New York City on her own. After being kicked out of her first apartment in New York, she was forced to live with a friend of hers until she was able to move back out on her own. Ameena attended school in Manhattan while also working two jobs in Queens. She later got a job in Soho; however, that job wasn't paying enough for her to be able to move out. At this point, she was contemplating moving back home to Atlanta.

One day at her job, she was stationed to take emails from all the customers. One specific lady had an unusual email, a company email. Being the bold person that Ameena is, she asked the lady where her email address was connected to, and the lady responded, "All employees get this email address when hired." Of course, Ameena asked if they were hiring, and the lady gladly said they were and then informed Ameena to send her a resumé that she would give directly to the hiring manager. Two weeks later, Ameena got hired making double the amount she had been making at her previous job. She now lives in a one-bedroom apartment in New York City and is finishing up her education, pursing her career in the film industry.

She told me without that miracle, she would have been staying with me. Oh, how I love unexpected support. When on your journey, things will fall in place or even seem coincidental to help you fulfill your desires.

The point of this story is to show that while unexpected support can be a breath of fresh air, it is only meant to be just that. We must continue to push forward. Support that comes from unexpected places is very important to our stage because it teaches us that we cannot do anything solely by ourselves. Once you open yourself up and begin to go in the direction of your dreams, you will see this happens from time to time. While it may seem like serendipity, believe it or not, these events were set in place from the beginning. You meet the right person at the right place at the right time. You begin to feel like your passion and work has not all been in vain. It can give you that extra push you need to keep going. Events start to take place that are unexpected and out of your control, but somehow seem to fit the mold for your journey of success. When this happens, don't discount it or chalk it up to coincidence. Instead, be very aware that it is a part of your journey to success and that you need to take full advantage of the experience in front of you.

Support from unexpected sources provides the breathing room we need while humbling us with the knowledge that there are genuine people out there who have vested interest in our personal well-being. As a child, I was taught by a close friend of the family that the best way to get success is to help as many people as you can to get there first. We all need support on our journey to success. Who will you lend a helping hand to?

Exercise: Throughout the day, find different situations that you have the power to solve. Get in the habit of solving problems and being there for someone when they least expect it, without any personal or financial gain. Every time you help someone out, at the end of the day write down what you did and how it helped that person. How did you feel afterwards, during, and before?

Affirmation: *I am a giver. I love to give freely because there is so much abundance in this world. I have more than enough to share.*

Chapter 7
The Setbacks

The next phase of the process on your journey to success is by far the longest and most important. *Pay attention to this chapter, because you are going to need it.* So far you have launched out into your dream, and you've discovered it to be a little bit harder than expected. Yet, you have pressed on and found help and support when you least expected it.

Life is great, and you are on your way to success. Then just when you think things are going smooth again, all hell breaks loose. Yes, that's right. You're not done. It's not over. YOU WILL ENOUNTER THIS STEP. It might happen quicker for some than for others, and each person will respond differently. The key is to prepare and elevate your mind so you can make it through.

In business, life, health, marriage, etc., there will be times when the pursuit of your dream flat out KICKS YOUR BUTT. I'm not talking about simple aggravation. This is where Murphy's Law comes into play. You get broken and bruised.

All the people you thought would be there aren't. No one who said they would be there is, and it seems like your dream is slipping from your grasp.

The primary purpose of this chapter is to stress the importance of what seems to be a very negative experience as an important step required to continue the journey to your success. This is one of the least expressed steps to the success track, but the most important. You will read different success stories that rarely draw the point of a setback. I will also explain a process you can use to help you get through this step.

Please understand it is imperative that when you are at this point, do not focus on the situation, but the results. Even if it seems that nothing is happening. At this point in the process, your emotions will be exposed and your ego will be crushed. You will learn how much success you're really meant to have, and you may even realize you're way in over your head. However, it is here you can determine your success, because if you don't give up, you will succeed. This is what I call "The Merlin Point in Life," where the things you truly want won't be a question of whether or not you can get it, but *how* you will get it. This will be one of the longest parts of your process.

The Chris Gardner story, which was later told in the inspiring movie *The Pursuit of Happyness* that was written by Steven Conrad, is a great story that really draws this point. In 1981 in San Francisco, Chris Gardner invests his family's savings in Osteo National bone-density scanners, a portable medical imaging device more expensive, but with a higher resolution than a traditional x-ray. The investment proves to be a white elephant (bad investment), which financially breaks the family, and as a result, his wife leaves him and their son, Christopher.

Chris is barely able to make ends meet through the occasional sale of one of the devices. One day while downtown, he meets a manager for Dean Witter and impresses him by solving a Rubiks Cube during a short cab ride. This new relationship earns him the chance to interview for a stockbroker internship that he is offered, but nearly turns down when the position turns out to be unpaid.

Chris is dealt a further setback when his bank account is garnished by the IRS for back taxes. He is unable to make his rent and is evicted from his apartment. Homeless, at one point, he is forced to stay in a bathroom at a public train station. He eventually finds the Glide Memorial United Methodist Church, which offers shelter to the homeless, but due to the demand for the limited room, he must leave work early every day in order to secure a place in line. Disadvantaged by his limited work hours, and knowing that maximizing his client contacts and profits is the only way to earn the one position that he and nineteen competitors are fighting for, Chris develops a number of ways to work more efficiently and reaches out to potential high-value customers defying protocol. Despite his personal challenges, he never reveals his circumstances to his co-workers, even going so far as to loan one of his bosses five dollars for a cab, a sum he can barely afford. At the end of his internship, Chris is called into a meeting with his managers. His struggle has paid off, and he is offered the position. Fighting back tears, he gratefully accepts. He rushes to his son's daycare, hugging him. Chris went on to form his own multi-million dollar brokerage firm.

This is one of the best true stories that describe a man who experienced major setbacks but persisted to move forward. Chris went from having a job and family to being homeless with his son and still fighting to reach the top. There are different levels in which we have to endure our setback, but it's a setback nonetheless.

During your journey to success, you will experience hardships, but you must keep going. To get through this part of the process, you create a habit of continual affirmation.

Murphy's Law says anything that can go wrong will go wrong. Although setbacks are temporary, they are MAJOR because this is the point where it becomes overwhelming. You are emotionally and physically drained.

Jerry Clark, the author of *Murphy's Committee,* says, "...when you start to pursue your dreams, you have to go through the 'jungle' in order to get to the greener side." In this jungle called life, you feel lost, you get unexpected surprises, and you can't see the light at the end of the tunnel. You have to fight to survive; you have to make the impossible happen. You have to come up with things that you don't have. You feel down, like you are at the lowest point of your life. You begin to question why you are going through this. At times, you feel like God has turned his back on you. It seems as if no one can understand where you are coming from. Everyone who stated they would help you out is not there. No one has your back anymore. At this point, you have to stay FOCUSED on the outcome. You have to focus on where you are going and keep your mind on the bigger goal.

Because your mind will be crowded by all sorts of things, it is important to have an outlined goal that you can focus on. You have to elevate your mind and see only your goal. This is where you go back to your exercises and affirmations from previous stages because you need those affirmations to push you through. You have to flood your brain with constant encouragement. This phase will hurt. All your weaknesses are revealed. This is hard for most people to swallow. Yet, once your weaknesses are revealed, you can see what you need to focus on. All your insecurities will be revealed and put to the test. The ego will have to be put in check because you may have to make sacrifices that you normally wouldn't. Depending on your circumstance, you may have to go from a Mercedes Benz to a less valued car, from gourmet food to Ramen noodles, from business owner to employee. You may not be able to live the life you had. You are forced to accept reality for what it really is. You have to accept what your current situation is. Your ego is put to the test as real-life situations take place. This is the longest process because it's the most gruesome. Going through this process allows you to build the thick skin that is necessary to continue.

It is designed by the law of nature to mold you into a vessel that could reach its fullest potential. The beauty behind the process is it's a requirement to attain success. How can you rise if you don't fall? If you keep sitting, you're not growing, but if you fall and get up, you are rising to your potential. Many people give up at this point. You decide whether you're supposed to have this much success. Some people are not meant to attain certain success, because again, success is measured in different ways.

While pledging for success, you may realize this is not what you wanted. So, you must go back to the beginning and reevaluate your goals and why you made them initially. Maybe you went after that particular dream for the wrong reason. Maybe that dream wasn't meant for you. In many cases, the dreamer may have misinterpreted what they thought about their dream. As weird as it sounds, that one person may not be the individual for that particular dream. Their whole pursuit may have been in vain. They could have been living their life based on someone else's pledge. That's why it is imperative when deciding to make a pledge that you research and perform a correct INNER VIEW.

How do you know if you're on the right path or not? Your *why* must be so strong that the *how* just falls into place. Only the person can determine this, because only the person can have an INNER VIEW. You are the only person that can have an INNER VIEW of yourself.

The key is to keep going. If you don't give up, you will tap into a force that will take you into another existence. Even if you decided that the path is not for you, you have not failed. It is okay, because you are now able to go back and find your destiny. Just keep going and harness the strength that becomes stronger than you. Just keep going! Focus on the positive from each situation. Your current thoughts dictate your future results.

The following is an interview I did that stresses the point of how a setback can condition us for bigger and better things—how small obstacles can lead to major rewards. Tiwa Aganga-Williams, known as TiwaWorks, is the CEO & President of The Celebrity Connect, an international booking company for A-List athletes, actors, entertainers, models, and public figures for private events, weddings, and concerts. TiwaWorks is the brand behind the Atlanta Greek Picnic, Inc., which is the biggest Divine Nine event in the country where all the historically black fraternities and sororities unite for a week of community service and social activities.

After interviewing Tiwa, the main thing he kept reiterating was that you must accept failure! Once you do, you will overcome your fear. You must get comfortable with failure in order to accept success. Tiwa explains, "One of the biggest lessons I learned was when I borrowed five thousand from an aunt to host a Rocafella event. At that time, five thousand was a lot for someone my age. I was responsible for every aspect of the event, from booking the artist and the venue to paying the door girl. Needless to say, the event flopped. I was forced to pay the loan back with money out of my pocket. After this experience, something in me numbed. I no longer feared failure. Preparing for failure caused me to be more tedious and pay more attention."

He is willing to take big risks now, which caused him to be more successful. Now his budget has gone from five thousand to sixty thousand, and even a hundred thousand in many cases.

Tiwa continued, "When I started doing the Atlanta Greek Picnic, I have to admit I was scared at first, but knowing that I must conquer the fear of failure in order to succeed allowed me to take that risk." It is now the biggest Divine Nine (the governing body of nine historically African-American Greek letter fraternities and sororities) event that each fraternity and sorority anticipates every year.

He says, "You become conditioned and learn how to let go of situations. You can't hold on to losses because you will never win. You have to prepare to lose in order to win. If you're not ready to lose, then you're not ready to win. You must accept failure as the platform to success." It is a skill to accept failure, but focus on the win.

Tiwa reminisced on a childhood movie that helped him grasp the concept of letting go. He states, "Even as a child, I was able to understand the importance of having faith. I remember watching *Indiana Jones and the Last Crusade*, where he tried to get the cup of life in order to save his father. He had to cross over what seemed to be a big drop. After sometime, he reflected on what his father had told him and took that first step of faith, and before you know it, he took another and was on the other side. I learned right then that you just have to take that first step to get to the next."

The following research is great because it really shows us the power of our thoughts, and in this negative time during the process, I feel it is important to understand how our brain functions with different challenges. It has been said by many that what we think about we bring about. So, really internalize this story and apply it to your way of thinking.

There was a study done by Dr. Masaru Emoto, who was born in Japan and graduated from Yokohama Municipal University and the Open International University as a Doctor of Alternative Medicine. His photographs were first featured in his self-published books *The Hidden Messages in Water 1 and 2. The Hidden Messages in Water* was first published in Japan, with over 400,000 copies sold internationally. What has put Dr. Emoto at the forefront of the study of water is his proof that thoughts and feelings affect physical reality. By producing different focused intentions through written and spoken words and music, and literally presenting it to the same water samples, the water appears to "change its expression".

Essentially, Dr. Emoto captured water's "expressions". He developed a technique using a very powerful microscope in a cold room, along with high-speed photography, to photograph newly formed crystals of frozen water samples. However, not all water samples crystallize. Water samples from extremely polluted rivers directly seem to express the "state" the water is in. Dr. Masaru Emoto discovered that crystals formed in frozen water reveal changes when specific, concentrated thoughts are directed toward them. He found that water from clear springs and water that has been exposed to loving words shows brilliant, complex, and colorful snowflake patterns. In contrast, polluted water, or water exposed to negative thoughts, forms incomplete, asymmetrical patterns with dull colors.

The implication of this research creates a new awareness of how we can positively impact the earth and our personal health. It has been stated that if thoughts can do that to bottles of water, imagine what our thoughts can do to our bodies, which are composed primarily of water.

Exercise: Write down everything you are grateful for and keep it in your pocket. The force of having something so powerful in your possession is an energy source in itself. The attitude of gratitude attracts prosperity.

Affirmation: The affirmation in this chapter will be in the form of a poem that can be found on the following page. This is the poem used around the world to express the point of continuing in time of struggle, of having strength when all odds seem against you. Therefore, I feel it's best to be this chapter's point of strength.

Invictus
By William Ernest Henley

Out of the night that covers me,
Black as the pit from pole to pole,
I thank whatever gods may be
For my unconquerable soul.
In the fell clutch of circumstance
I have not winced nor cried aloud.
Under the bludgeonings of chance
My head is bloody, but unbowed.
Beyond this place of wrath and tears
Looms but the horror of the shade,
And yet the menace of the years
Finds and shall find me unafraid.
It matters not how strait the gate,
How charged with punishments the scroll,
I am the master of my fate:
I am the captain of my soul.

Chapter 8
Learning to Let Go

The beauty of going through hard times is that after a while, it becomes so tiresome that you literally give up trying. You give up trying to swim upstream, and you just let go. In this chapter, I will explain the art of letting go. Do not take this chapter literally. Letting go is a mental process. Everything happens inside first, and then it is translated outside.

Also, letting go does not mean just sitting there and letting something happen. You can't simply say, "I'm just going to sit here and think about what I want." That statement is wrong because there is a big thing called ACTION that is required in order for anything to take place. In order for you to attract that million dollars in your life, or whatever goal you are trying to attain, let go of the thought of wanting it. Knowing it's already here will allow it to flow into your life easier. All you need is the necessary steps to move towards it. In order for you to attract that lunch you are so hungry to eat, you can let go of the thought of wanting it. Lunch isn't magically going to appear because you want it. Action is required in everything. This is the same concept of the snowball rolling down the hill. You can't just think about it. You have to take the action of pushing the snowball in the first place. Letting go requires thought and then action. Take this chapter from an emotional sense and you will gain more from it.

Now, the concept behind letting go is deeper than you think. If you have ever been whitewater rafting, you know it makes no sense to push upstream because you're pushing against the current. That is pretty much how life flows. We are all trying to get to the top, and the best way to do it is not to push against the current. The current is the metaphor for life, and the raft is the body that we are in. The beauty behind that concept is as we flow with the current of life, we are forced to work within the parameters set by the water because the water is the controlling force. We have to steer and guide while going down the current. When we begin to just go with the flow, you wind up going in the direction you need to go.

When letting while experiencing difficulties, or when you feel like you are about to give up, everybody has a "this is too much for me" moment. It's when they think, "I've overestimated myself, and you know what? Forget it." Pay attention to this: When you get to that point, at that very moment if you just let go, I can almost guarantee that things are going to go smoother.

Have you ever wanted something really bad, and then when you don't care anymore, it just falls into your lap? That is the same concept of letting go. For example, when you know you need something and you don't know how it's going to come to you, and you stop stressing over it by saying, "It is what it is," it suddenly seems like things just fall into place. This happens because you let it go into the universe, and you let the universe know that you are going to let it do its job. You are not going to do anything else. You take yourself and your ability out of the equation and let God be God.

When overwhelming adversity comes, you have to see it for what it is. Accept that it is going to come, and then let it go and flow with the current of life. No eagle can fly until you kick it out of the nest. In the animal kingdom, when a mother feels it is time for her child to grow up and take on life, she refuses them milk. Some species even take their cubs into the wilderness and leave them there, forcing the young cub to fight his own battles and find his way home.

Adversity is a part of life. The best you can do is to do what you know how to do and then let God have his way, not your way. Don't focus on your thought process. Don't try to reanalyze your ideas. Please understand that no man can outwit the universe. What is meant to happen will happen. When you plant a seed, you have to let it grow. You can't keep picking it up to see if it's going to grow. You can't stand over it all night, sweating and stressing over the seed, and then pick it back up and examine it to come up with your own shortcuts for growth. You have to plant it and leave it alone. The important part is it's been planted. You then have to let life do the rest.

Letting go does not mean just giving up after you have tried and seemingly gotten no results. To let go, you have to let go of the STRESS and the EGO that comes along with wanting what you want when you want it.

For example, my mother was in a very controlling relationship to the point where she thought she did not have her independence or her own voice. In some instances, when you go for so long without dictating, you feel like you have no power.

However, when she decided to let go and be happy within herself, she became free and decided to leave that situation. Have you ever been in a situation where you thought all hell was breaking loose and there seemed to be no way out? Don't allow the circumstance to control you. Let's just admit it. For some of us, it's easier to stress because stressing makes you feel like you are contributing to the situation. It makes you think you are on top of things, as if you have an eye on the situation. As children, we see people stress, and we think a stressed-out person is in charge. But, that's not the case at all. Letting go is a hard concept to grasp, and it's not something that happens overnight. You have to get yourself to accept things are taking place, and let them be.

Once you grasp the concept that life flows, it makes things a lot easier. When you breathe, do you think about inhaling and exhaling, or do you just do it? Do you stress about it? Even as you're reading these words on this page, how do you distinguish between "I'm in control" and "I'm allowing"? The irony of letting go in regards to pledging for success is when you let go, your dream comes faster. Look at it this way: The purpose of Chapters 1-7 is to prepare you for the moment when you let go, when you allow your dream to take place.

As human beings, we are here to live and let live. We have to be forced to let go. Letting go cannot happen without annoyance. Otherwise, you are not really letting go. If you don't have trouble or anxiety, then what are you letting go of? When you learn to let go, you become immune to the struggle. You become immune to problems. Whatever happens, happens. And if you don't give it any attention, it doesn't exist! All the issues that are problems are only because we make them issues. It becomes a perception of our current reality, but our problems are only as big as the weight we give them. The moment we decide that we don't want to create a monster, we let go.

WHAT YOU DON'T PUT NEGATIVE EMOTIONAL THOUGHT ON DOES NOT EXIST. We have to learn to sensor what thoughts we want to intake. The longer you think about it, the more you create. Saying, thinking, and acting negatively creates exactly what you say or think. For example, when people vent, instead of venting about what is wrong, vent on what is about to go right. What you focus on is what you get. So, focus on what you want! It can start during childhood when we learn that if we go to our mommy with a problem, she will fix it. If we complain, make a scene, or cry, then it will be attended to. However, that is not the way to get your prayer answered, because people have situations they are going through, as well, and they don't want to hear you complaining. Let it go. Let go of the negativity. Live in every moment positively.

Here is how you practice letting go. Here is how you become good at it. Whenever you begin to bombard the mind with your negative situations, ask yourself, "Where am I right now?" Every moment you're in is unique, and all you have is that current moment. All the problems you think have taken place are only illusions of what you think may happen. Yet, that's not the moment you're in right now, so the problem technically doesn't matter.

Our mind is very creative. We can create a whole reality. Someone can be sitting in a room for a week and create a story of negativity that will keep them from leaving that room. For instance, if they step out, they may get attacked, and they believe it. The brain is a very powerful thing. We have to learn to control it, and the best way to do it is letting go. Don't try to have your hands in every cookie jar. Just let things exist. It's going to happen with or without you. You can't control it. You're not this special force. You are not the controller of everything. By you letting go, you control it.

For example, some people say, "If I want to walk from point A to point B, I can do so. Therefore, I'm in control." I would say, "Who told you to get up and walk? Who explained to you that if you put one foot in front of the other, you will walk. Is it something you think about or do?" Of course, that person would then answer, "Duh! I just do it." If you just do it, then you let go, because when you think about walking, you actually find yourself beginning to stutterstep.

Pledging for success teaches you to let go. It should be called pledging to let go. I saw my mother for her birthday, and she had this glow. She said she was learning the art of letting go and things were happening for her! She was getting clients, meeting the right people at the right time. She received the right phone call at the right time. How do we justify that? How do you? You can't. That's just the way it is. Just let go.

Now, on the contrary, learning to let go does not mean giving up. In many cases, at this point in the pledge process, people do give up. Letting go does not mean you say, "You know what? Forget it. I'm just not going to handle responsibilities and watch things take place."

Letting go is a mental state that effects your physical situation. You still have to go with the flow of life. You still have to continue your personal regiment, but it's the thoughts that go with it. Pay your bills, but let go of the attachment to its burden. You can't quit your job, but you can let go of your negativity towards your job and use it as a vessel to focus on where you want to go. Letting go is a concept. Don't drop out of school. By letting go, you say, "I'm going to change the way I view this class. I'm going to stop attaching so much negativity to it." The same applies to the current of a river. If you jump out of the raft, you drown. Letting go is not dropping your oars. It's the decision to ride the current. You need to stay on board, stay inside the boat, and ride the current to where you are going.

Letting go means not allowing your current situation to control your life. You have to practice releasing the tension that your obstacle is giving you. By doing so, it allows your head to clear up and leaves room for ideas to flood your brain.

Exercise: Simply LET GO! This is probably the hardest exercise you will encounter throughout this entire book.

Affirmation: *God, grant me the Serenity to accept things I cannot change, the Courage to change the things I can, and the Wisdom to know the difference. Written by Reinhold Niebuhr*

Chapter 9
The Crossing Over

At this point, you are feeling good. You have everything you prayed for; the dream came true. You are excited because you have finally crossed over. You feel like a new person. **No one goes through a process without changing.** You start seeing things differently. You accept things in a different light. You are no longer the same person. You're now (INSERT YOUR NAME), the SUCCESS.

This is a "feel good" chapter. The crossing over is the transition to the next level in your life. The change has taken place. Have you ever wanted something so bad that you practically talked about it all the time, and when you finally got it, a certain feeling came across you that just illuminated your world? Well, that feeling is what this chapter is about—how to recognize that you've crossed over. Many people live in fear that the journey to success has no happy ending. Then why pursue it? It's the happy feeling that we want so much that allows us to continue. I will also discuss the importance of our emotions. Learning to focus on the greater emotions can be an asset when going through our journey.

My sophomore year in college, I applied to audition for the Julliard Performance Arts School. During this time, I had only acted for two years and had no actual training, but my good friend Amari attended the school and suggested I audition. I remember choosing my two monologues for the audition and being scrutinized for selecting a Shakespeare piece because that school is well versed in Shakespeare. I was told my audition would be judged harder.

Audition day was just like what you see on television, a couple hundred people in the halls waiting their turn. I remember feeling intimidated because I overheard other students stating it was their third time auditioning and how much training they had done. There was even one guy who was sure he would get selected because his family was "connected".

There were about eight different rooms and different time slots. It bothered me as to how they made their selections with so many different rooms and people, but I couldn't judge their process. I walked in my class where there were three professors sitting in the back of the room. After I introduced myself, they told me to begin. When I was done, they thanked me and sent me out of the room. I can't explain how fast the process was, but it was quick. I was instructed to come back in the room, which seemed unusual, but they wanted me to redo my Shakespeare monologue of *Hamlet*. I thought, *Man, I was warned about this. Now they're about to dissect my performance.* They asked me to show them the two different voices in the 'To Be Or Not To Be" monologue. Seeing a chair on the side, I asked to use it. With each different voice, I changed seats. Once again, they thanked and dismissed me. I was told I had to wait until the end of the day to see the results.

Later that evening, all the students were in the hall anxiously waiting. The tension was so obvious it was uncomfortable. A lady finally came out of the room with a sheet of paper and said, "If your name is on this list, please stand by for further information." I can remember this like it was yesterday. I was across from where she posted the paper, but wasn't able to fully read it. I paused because all I saw were four names and students walking away disappointed. I finally mustered up the courage to walk over and read the paper. My name was number three on the sheet. My heart dropped. That was one of the best feelings I ever felt. It's that moment where everything around you stops, and your primary focus is on what just took place. That's what it feels like to cross over. I ended up not going to the school, but the feeling to me was just as rewarding.

When you get that dream and it comes true, you feel light as a feather. You have a full understanding that even though you will have obstacles, there is nothing in life that you can't achieve. The struggles you had make things easier for you. Success is a journey that you must go through; it's a journey that will lead you to your goal. I was taught that everything happens for a reason, and that when you fall, just pick yourself up and keep going. Success is when you fall and fall, but no matter how many times you keep falling you get back up. At that moment when you get up and finally achieve your goal, then you have achieved success.

Now what emotions were going through your head as you read that statement? If you actually visualized yourself falling and getting back up, you may have felt a since of pride and strength for not staying down, and at the end when you

FINALLY achieved your goal, you became someone. You felt a sense of pride. Those frozen moments in time when you are successful, you tell yourself, "WOW! I finally made it." Now this could be toward anything—a baseball game, cooking, grades, whatever. It's not the situation I am referring to. It's the actual feeling that comes with that situation.

Emotions are one of the best ways to remember events in our life. Once you have experienced a strong life changing emotion, you can conjure it up whenever you want. Good and bad. Try to recapture the moment when you failed and it really affected you. How did you feel? Go ahead and think about that moment right now. How precise is that feeling? Now, if I were to ask you to remember the first time you ate a burger and remember the exact emotion you felt, that may be a little difficult for most of us because it doesn't mold how we do things today.

Our emotions have a lot more power than we think. Understanding the power of emotions allows us the freedom to choose which emotion we want to focus on. **The emotions that you can conjure up right now are the emotions you can easily change.** In order for us to change the emotions that mold how we live today is to recognize that this emotion is unwanted. In order to fully understand this concept, we would have to really internalize whatever it is we are trying to achieve. It's our thought about something that we can control.

For example, if we have a vision of reaching the top of a mountain, we would already have had to reach it in our minds in order to reach it physically. Events in our lives have already happened before we are consciously aware of it. It's like a lightning bolt. We see the lightning before we hear the thunder. The humorous part about this concept is that we do it every day, all day unconsciously. Everything you want starts as a thought—every action, every decision, everything. We just have to go through the physical movements to manifest the thought.

Stop looking at what you want to do as a struggle. You are capable of it. Stop looking at where you want to go as an obstacle. The destination is within your grasp. What we think about, we bring about. You must begin looking at the things you do completely different. There is no such thing as you can't do it, because success is never-ending. To put it in a better perspective, it is as if there is an apple in your hand and you are begging for one. It's already in your hand. Can you not feel it?

The following excerpt was taken from Jack Canfield's *The Success Principles.* "Around 1990, when Jim Carrey was a struggling young Canadian comic trying to make his way in Los Angeles, he drove his old Toyota up to Mulholland Drive. While sitting there looking at the city below and dreaming of his future, he wrote himself a check for ten million dollars, dated it Thanksgiving 1995, and added the notation 'for acting services rendered', and then he carried it in his wallet from that day forth. The rest, as they say, is history. Carrey's optimism and tenacity eventually paid off, and by 1995, after the huge box office success of *Ace Ventura: Pet Detective, The Mask,* and *Dumb & Dumber*, his asking price had risen to twenty million dollars per picture. When Carrey's father died in 1994, he placed the ten-million-dollar check into his father's coffin as a tribute to the man who had both started and nurtured his dreams of being a star."

Just gives you something to think about regarding the power of visualization, affirmations, and having clearly defined goals, doesn't it? The key is to know that it has already happened and walk around with that conviction.

Exercise: Congrats! Exercise pass! Celebrate! Stay focused! Enjoy your exercise pass.

Affirmation: *I create miracles with my thoughts.*

Chapter 10
The Change

You have now completed the process, and your experience of going through it has caused you to change. Have you ever heard someone say when you get money you will change? Or when someone gets a new job or car they changed? Basically, when you acquire a new goal, you change, because the process that you went through forces you to change. Whenever you wear your badge of success or have the new job or promotion, the friends you have will say you are no longer the person that they used to know. They will say you are acting brand new. The truth is you are. If you went through a process, you will change. It is impossible to go through a process and not change. A prime example is when you lose weight. You no longer can wear the same clothes or eat the same things. You are forced to change because nothing is the same anymore. Everything about you changes because you have been shaped by the dream. You are no longer (INSERT YOUR NAME). You are now (INSERT YOUR NAME), the SUCCESS or whatever dream you have accomplished.

The biggest thing most people fear is that they may be judged for the change that took place. Who you are won't change. Your awareness will change. How you handle things will change because now you are aware of what to expect in life. You are now prepared for whatever is to come.

Don't worry how people see you. They will see you differently. You may not have the same friends that you had in the beginning of your journey. It will become harder because people can't appreciate what you have been through since they have not gone through it. That is why "rich" people don't just give their money to anyone. It wasn't given to them, and they know they will be doing that person an injustice by bailing them out and interrupting that person's pledge for success. As easy as it was given it can be just as easily taken. If you haven't pledged for it, it's hard for you to appreciate it.

For example, my older sister has been in the medical field for quite some time now, and she always tells the same story of two women. One had a triple bypass surgery, and the other went on an extraneous diet. The purpose of her story is to emphasize how going through an extraneous process will benefit you in the long run, as opposed to taking the easy way out. She stated that the woman who had bypass surgery was more than likely to gain the weight back over a few short months because she didn't work hard to lose the weight. She just had a few short surgeries, and therefore, she doesn't know how to maintain it or appreciate it. It's the stomach stapling that keeps them from eating more food; there is no willpower. As opposed to the person who works really hard, and it took them a year or more to lose the weight. They know what it takes to reach their goal, and they don't want to risk gaining the weight back because they worked so hard to lose it. Now, both situations will change you, but one will be long lasting and have a permanent affect. If she was to ever gain some pounds, it would be a lot easier for her to lose it because she already knows what it takes to do so.

You become a different person; your dream shapes you into an athlete. You are shaped into this awareness of self that no one else will understand because only you went through the process, it's personal.

Rapper 50 Cent said it best. "The person that says money doesn't change them hasn't made enough." Your possessions change you not because of the possession, but because of the process it took for you to get it.

If you are not a new person, then you have not pledged for success. It's not a moment of saying, "Okay, I guess I'm successful." You KNOW it. You can feel it all over your body. You do things completely different. Pledging for success creates a blueprint for your life that you can always reference. It's like your own personal success model that you personally created. It becomes ingrained in your D.N.A. Once you do it, it just flows, and that's what it means to be changed by the success.

You form into this persona that is different than you were before. Butterflies are a great example. There are four stages in the life cycle of a butterfly: the egg, larva or caterpillar, pupa or chrysalis, and the adult. I will break down each stage as it relates to the process.

Briefly, a butterfly starts as an egg. *This can be considered the beginning stages of your journey.* After about three to five days (some species take up to three weeks), the egg hatches and a tiny caterpillar (larva) emerges. *Now your dreams have taken form, and you can fully see the goal.* Then the caterpillar starts to eat and will shed its skin four to six times as it gets bigger.

After about two to five weeks, the caterpillar will be full-grown and transform itself into a pupa/chrysalis. *It would appear that you have achieved a major goal, that you have reached the fullest form. But, not yet. The setback has to take place.* Inside the pupa, the caterpillar's body breaks down into a kind of soup from which grows the adult structure of the butterfly! This stage can take between ten to fifteen days. *What appears to be the death of the butterfly is actually the transformation that is needed to grow into a beautiful species.* Finally, the adult butterfly emerges from the chrysalis. Adult butterflies will mate, the female will lay eggs, and the life cycle starts over. The whole process is called metamorphosis, which means change of form. (*http://www.flmnh.ufl.edu/butterflies/qanda.html*)

Without being fully aware of these stages, many would believe that once it enters the pupa stage, the butterfly is dying out. Instead, it's going through a process which is required to transform into something beautiful. Expect change. Expect to be ridiculed, because no one can understand the process you went through. So, don't expect to be understood.

This is the best poem that can sum this chapter up. Really internalize these words.

"Our deepest fear is not that we are inadequate. Our deepest fear is that we are powerful beyond measure. It is our light, not our darkness, that frightens us most. We ask ourselves, 'Who am I to be brilliant, gorgeous, talented, and famous?' Actually, who are you not to be? You are a child of God. Your playing small does not serve the world. There is nothing enlightening about shrinking so that people won't feel insecure around you. We were born to manifest the glory of God that is within us. It's not just in some of us. It's in all of us. And when we let our own light shine, we unconsciously give other people permission to do the same. As we are liberated from our own fear, our presence automatically liberates others."

Written by Miran Williamson
Used by Nelson Mandela in his 1994 inaugural speech

Exercise: List all your talents, attributes, and your gifts so that whenever you get discouraged or start to question who you are, you can go back to that list and remember why you are special. Don't be afraid of changing into something better just because someone else is afraid of taking that first step. Not everyone will achieve greatness, so be proud that you did.

Affirmation: *I am who I am, and that's okay.*

Chapter 11
You Must Keep Growing

It's true what they say; it takes money to make money. It's also true what they say about success attracting success. So you've changed and you're on the track of success, but it doesn't stop there.

The dream becomes bigger than you anticipated. You have been changed. It starts to take a life of its own where it flourishes into something huge.

Then the danger zone presents itself, and you have an option. You can get scared by it, or you can decide to move on. It becomes a situation where you must make a decision to go back through the pledge process in order to move forward. The danger zone is where the person may not be prepared or become content. They achieve success so quickly that they don't know how to handle it. This is when you have to have another INNER VIEW with yourself to see if you want to keep going.

This chapter is about what you must do next after achieving your goal. A lot of us only focus on the current goal, but can be clueless as to what's next when we have accomplished that goal. It's very simple. You must keep dreaming. Many people in business face that decision, and sometimes it becomes overwhelming. The danger zone in pledging for success is when you've arrived. You can either become a t-shirt wearer (just living off your title) or actually do what you said you would do–carry on the image you have created and stand by what you built. You can either just wear the success symbol, or you can actually become a doer and do what is expected of you. Others just live off the perceptions of what they have accomplished.

While in the danger zone, you can pretend or you can actually live what you are. You have to make the decision to make a pledge, but this time, you are prepared because you know what is expected. People are afraid to continue their pledge because there is always a struggle. *Problems lead to solutions, and solutions lead to a goal.* Success is a never-ending journey, just like a moving train. The process is to get on that train, but the train is going to keep going. Don't jump off. Sometimes the train runs off the track, but you have to really be prepared for this thing called success. The danger of reaching success is not knowing how to handle it or what to do when you receive it. The best way to handle it is to reminisce on the process.

Keep allowing yourself to go through the process. Because you already have the blueprint for your success, you will be okay. Don't let someone come in with a crayon and create a whole new direction for you. You already have your blueprint for success; it becomes a part of your instincts. We have it naturally. As we grow older, we attain wisdom, which increases our instinct.

The hard part of the danger zone is to know you're in it and not be afraid to go through it like you did with everything else. You will always be pledging for success. What makes it easier every time you do it is the awareness you are actually pledging. You get better at seeing what part of the process you're at. This allows you to anticipate at which points you can move forward. The dreamer has to create new dreams. You can either get comfortable, scared, or settle, or you can create a bigger dream. Now that you understand the different steps of pledging for success, it should be awareness in your head which allows you to understand why each step is required. Use this as a map to your journey. Some of you may already be on the road, but knowing where you are will help you push through. It's like driving the same route to work every morning. Because you already know what is up ahead, it makes the drive faster.

Exercise: Take out a sheet of paper and write down how much money you plan on making in three years and place the number here: _____. Now, add three more zeros to that number, and that's how much you should be making. Now, write down all the possible thoughts that came to your mind when you saw that number. Focus on those thoughts. If negative, tackle them right now. If positive, make it grow. Have a book by the side of your bed with a pen already in it. Every morning when you wake up, write all possible dreams that could benefit you in it. Write down all your dreams and call it your dream book.

Affirmation: *I always, always dream BIG!*

Made in the USA
Charleston, SC
13 November 2011